CW00472348

Fantasy Coloring
BY ELINA

For more fantasy coloring
visit my website
HTTPS://FANTASYCOLORING.COM/

Your opinion is important to me.

THANK YOU FOR CHOOSING MY FANTASY COLORING BOOK AND SUPPORTING ME.

I HOPE YOU HAVE AS MUCH FUN COLORING AS I HAD CREATING IT.

PLEASE LEAVE A REVIEW ON AMAZON AND SHARE SOME OF YOUR COLORED PICTURES WITH ME AND OTHERS.

ENJOY THE MYSTERIES OF THE FANTASY UNDERWATER WORLD NOBODY HAS SEEN BEFORE.

This book belongs to:

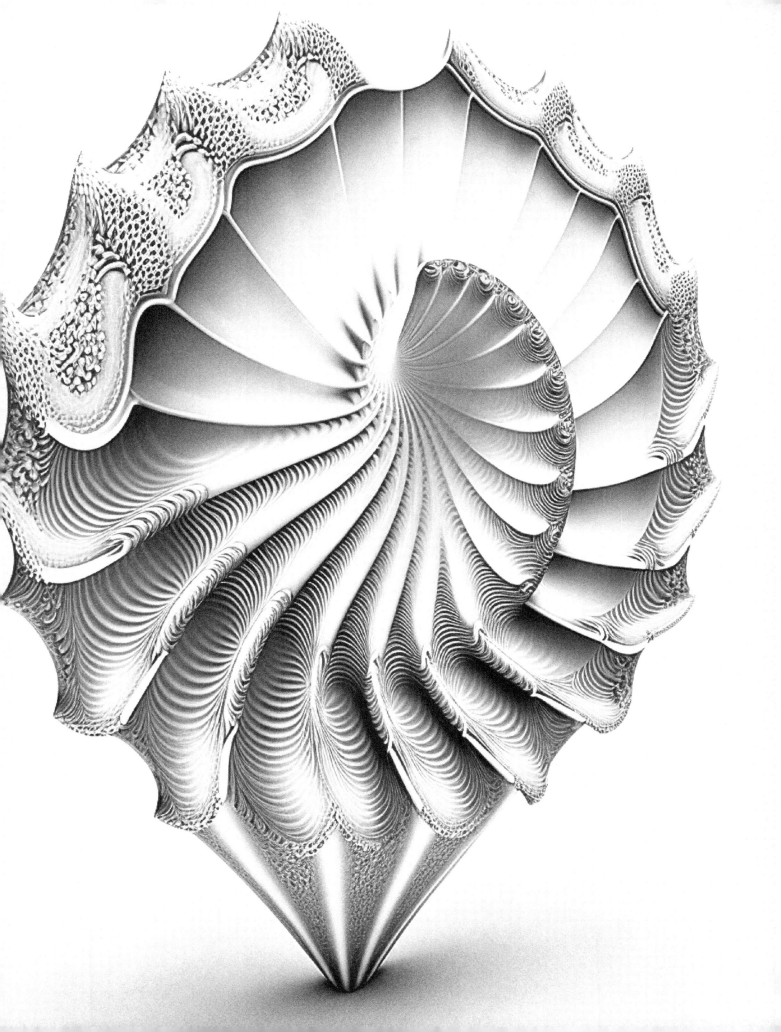

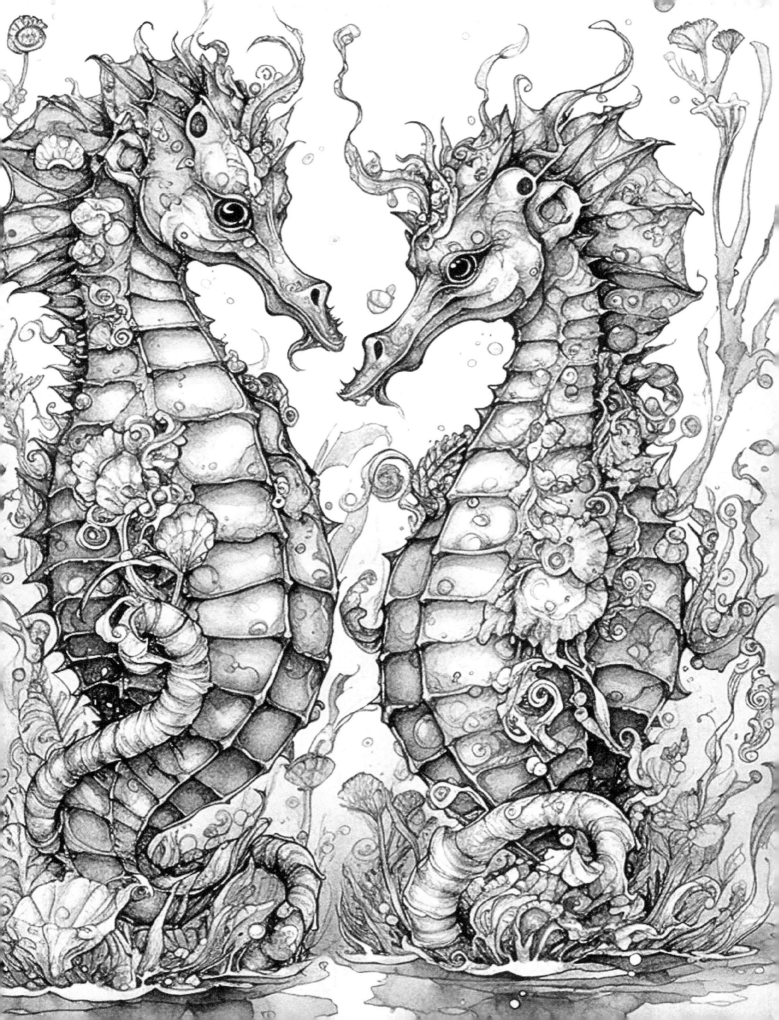

Printed in Great Britain
by Amazon

21479664R00038